C000259729

IMAGES
of Wales

BUTETOWN AND CARDIFF DOCKS

'Tiger Bayee, Tiger Bayee, its not very far from the docks. Once you get to Loudoun Square take the first turning there, Tiger Bayee, Tiger Bayee, Tiger Bayee'
The above song was sung in docklands pubs to the tune of Goodbyee,
a First World War song.

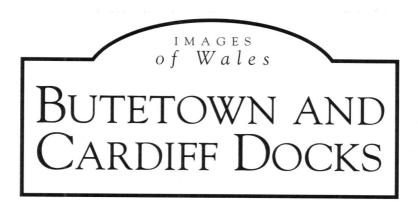

IMAGES
of Wales

BUTETOWN AND
CARDIFF DOCKS

Compiled by
Brian Lee and Butetown History and Arts Centre

Butetown History & Arts Centre
The Bay People's Story

TEMPUS

First published 1999
Copyright © Brian Lee and Butetown History and Arts Centre, 1999

Tempus Publishing Limited
The Mill, Brimscombe Port,
Stroud, Gloucestershire, GL5 2QG

ISBN 0 7524 1582 4

Typesetting and origination by
Tempus Publishing Limited
Printed in Great Britain by
Midway Clark Printing, Wiltshire

Contents

Foreword

I am delighted to be asked to write the foreword to this book. Butetown and the docks have been absolutely crucial to the development of Cardiff as a major world port and have been at the heart of its modern history.

The unique multicultural area of Butetown is not only a part of my constituency, it is where I worked professionally within the community immediately before entering Parliament, so the people and the area are very special to me.

This book, with its evocative collection of photographs, most of which are from the Butetown History and Arts Centre archive, with text by Brian Lee, will delight readers for many years to come.

The Rt Hon Alun Michael JP, MP
Secretary of State for Wales
Honorary President of Butetown History and Arts Centre

Introduction

Early nineteenth-century Cardiff was still a small town, largely untouched by the Industrial Revolution. Its development as a major port began with the opening of the first stage of the Bute Docks complex in 1839. This was quite an event with thousands lining the procession route from Cardiff Castle to the dock. The parade included mud labourers, masons, dockworkers, tradesmen, schoolchildren, police, bands, all with flags and banners, as well as the Marquis of Bute who formally took possession of the dock. The first ship to sail into the dock was the *Lady Charlotte* steamer. The proximity of Cardiff to the sea and its natural harbour made it an ideal site for development, and the extension of the Taff Vale Railway line gave the coal fields of south Wales, for the first time, a direct route to the sea. The first train load of Rhondda steam coal, which was to dominate the south Wales coal producing area, reached Cardiff on 17 December 1855.

By the 1890s Cardiff was Britain's largest coal exporting port, with exports peaking at over 10 million tons in 1913. The expansion of the port attracted British and international capital, symbolized most prominently in Mount Stuart Square by the famous Coal and Shipping Exchange. These industrialists, merchants and speculators invested heavily in the industries which contributed to the growth of the docklands.

Cardiff became the centre of the coal exporting trade and the Coal Exchange, built in 1886, was the base for all coal trade, not just that which was shipped through Cardiff. Cardiff Docks also became a major centre for ship repairing – ships entering Cardiff in ballast could be dry-docked for repairs before proceeding to the wet docks to load new cargoes. To supplement the ship repairing and coal exporting industries there emerged a multitude of ancillary industries around the dock area including ships' chandlers, canvas and ropeworks, shops and chemists. The Dowlais Steel Works opened at East Moors in 1891. This move reduced transport costs giving the company direct access to the point of export and the locally manufactured steel was readily available to the ship repairing industry. More docks had to be built to keep pace with the constantly expanding trade, culminating in 1907 with the opening of the 52 acre Queen Alexandra Dock.

Migrant workers, who moved there to build and work the docks, increased in the population of Cardiff rapidly, contributing to the development of the unique cosmopolitan community of Butetown. Many of Cardiff's nineteenth-century immigrants were Irish and by the 1840s there was a thriving Irish community in Newtown. In the mid-1800s, the residential area of Butetown was built. As owners of most of the land in Cardiff, the Bute family had a great deal of control over building and they were happy for the residential and commercial area which grew up around the docks to be called 'Butetown'. It was the intention of the Bute estate that the area be occupied by people of different class backgrounds. However, this intended socially and economically mixed development was short-lived. The middle classes, including sea captains, pilots, merchants, builders, managers, moved out as the new suburbs developed and the public transport system extended.

The area came to house a cosmopolitan working class community. People from Great Britain and Ireland, Europe, the Middle East, the Far East, Africa and the Americas, most of them seamen and their families, lived in harmony, for the most part, in that insulated island which became known worldwide as 'Tiger Bay'.

From the early 1800s to the Second World War people from more than fifty countries settled in Cardiff's docklands. Most of the immigrants were male and, once here, they met and often married women from the south Wales valleys and other parts of the British Isles, many of whom had been attracted to Cardiff by the prospect of domestic work in the expanding service sector. Intermarriage between diverse ethnic groups made for a community rich in culture and understanding. These people and their descendants worked on the tramp steamers and dredgers, in the dry docks and dock sides, in the steelworks and factories and in the offices and shops. Cardiff's industrial and maritime history was largely built by their hard work.

Industrial decline since the Second World War has led to great changes in Butetown and the dockland area – not the least, the redevelopment of the 1950s and '60s when most of the Victorian buildings were demolished to make way for the new post-war housing developments. The houses in Loudoun Square, built in the style of the great London squares around a large iron railed garden, were demolished and the two tower blocks which occupy the site of that garden now dominate the skyline. The dock area now houses the new residential and commercial communities of 'Cardiff Bay'. Little is left but memories of the grandeur that was Cardiff Docks.

However, still to be seen are the early gated houses of Bute Crescent and a few original houses in Mount Stuart Square, now used for commercial purposes. Bute Esplanade, Windsor Terrace and Windsor Esplanade at the foreshore are largely as they were, and still family dwellings. A walk in this area will give the visitor a glimpse of what has gone before. For the rest this book will help evoke memories and give the reader a taste of what it was like to live and work in Butetown and the docks.

Molly Maher
Research and Archive Officer
Butetown History and Arts Centre

One
Dockland Scenes

The West Dock was the first dock to be opened on 9 October 1839.

'The days of the old windjammers – otherwise sailing ships – seem to have left us forever. Often as a boy I have stood on Cardiff Pier Head and witnessed the sailing of long ships.' A correspondent gave this account when writing to the *Cardiff & Suburban News* in 1927.

The East Basin of Cardiff Bute Docks, *c.* 1890.

The *Swan of Bideford*, which was built in 1797, is seen here leaving Bute Docks. Mount Stuart Hotel can be seen to the left of the picture.

A crowd gathered at the entrance to the Bute West Dock, *c.* 1890.

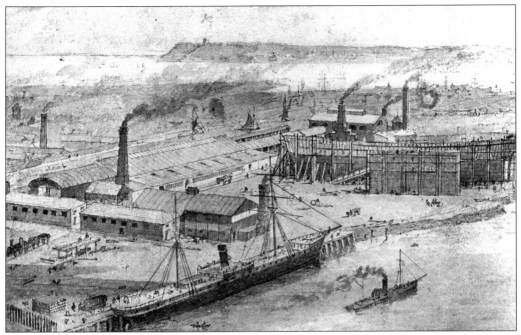

The shipbuilding yard on Clarence Road, *c.* 1884.

The premises of Batchelor Brothers, shipbuilders, *c.* 1859.

Sailing ships were still in vogue when this picture was taken, *c.* 1870.

Captain Scott's ship, *Terra Nova*, sailed out of Cardiff Docks heading for the South Pole on the British Antarctic Expedition in 1910.

Working at the docks could be backbreaking work. These local women are unloading potatoes at England's Wharf, *c*. 1905.

The entrance to Cardiff Docks, *c*. 1900.

The Pier Head building, designed in French Gothic style by William Frame, housed the offices of the Bute Dock Company.

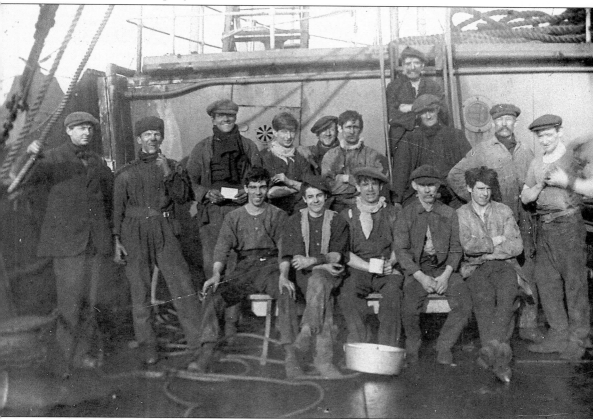

Seamen had a hard time at the turn of the century, when this picture was taken. But these unknown seamen looked happy enough when they posed for this picture.

The grandest building on the waterfront, the Exchange, was badly damaged by fire in 1829. Later rebuilt and extended, it was bought by the Powell Duffryn Colliery Company, *c*. 1902.

Powell Duffryn House is to the right of the picture, which is looking North to Bute Street, *c*. 1902.

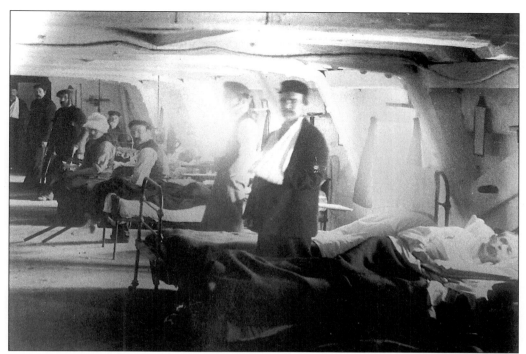

Patients aboard the HMS *Hamadryad* hospital ship, *c*. 1870.

The HMS *Hamadryad* was towed from Plymouth and berthed in Cardiff East Dock as a seamen's hospital which opened on 1 November 1866.

The HMS *Havannah* sailed into Cardiff East Bute Dock in 1860. It was later converted to an industrial school known as the Cardiff Ragged School and was berthed near Penarth Bridge.

The frigate HMS *Thisbe* was loaned by the Admiralty for the purpose of becoming a mission church to seamen which opened at the East Bute Dock on 13 August 1863.

Five seamen aboard the tug *Riflemen* were killed when the vessel exploded at the entrance to Bute Dock in 1886.

The *Yewgarth*, run aground.

Ships berthed in the West Docks Basin, *c.* 1912.

Awaiting attention in the Commercial Dry Dock is the London ship *Sapphire*, *c.* 1912.

In 1897 the Channel Dry Docks and Engineering Company Ltd was incorporated. A dry dock 630ft long, with a 64ft entrance was constructed.

The *Wiltshire*, a gas carrier, is seen here in Cardiff Docks.

The SS *George Washington* visited Cardiff Docks on 29 July 1928.

Work on the Morecambe Lifebuoy in the Channel Dry Dock nearing completion, *c*. 1970.

The timber on this ship came from Finland. Other imports of timber to Cardiff came from Russia, Scandinavia and Newfoundland.

Timber imports to Cardiff dated back to around 1813. Robinson, David & Company Ltd, pictured here, distributed timber to all parts of the country.

'When Coal was King'. An impressive sight in the coal marshalling yards in Cardiff Docks, c. 1940.

Traverser coal hoists at Queen Alexandra Docks are seen here before the Second World War.

The first service of electric tramcars commenced between City Road (then called Castle Road) and the docks in 1902.

Docks policemen, *c.* 1895.

This photograph was taken when paddle steamers ran every twenty minutes from Cardiff Docks to Penarth Pier, *c.* 1880.

Pleasure steamers have operated in the Bristol Channel for more than one hundred years.

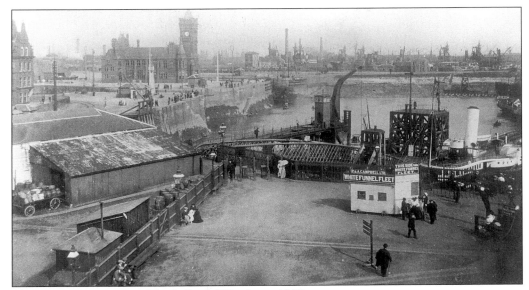

Pleasure steamers at Pier Head, Cardiff Docks, *c*. 1900.

The Pier Head building in the background opened in 1897 as the headquarters of the Cardiff Railway Company.

Children from Cardiff Waifs and Strays Society leaving Cardiff.

Esso Preston, Cardiff Docks, *c.* 1950.

During the Second World War, women worked as porters for the Great Western Railway at Cardiff Docks.

Mount Stuart Dry Dock, *Techniquest*, was built on the site to the left of the picture and Lansea House, on the right, seen here around 1970, now houses Harry Ramsden's fish restaurant.

Two
Shops and Businesses

Reg Crabtree standing outside his hairdresser's salon in Stuart Street in 1967.

Patterson's the butchers in James Street was established in 1848. This picture was taken in 1920.

Patterson's butcher's shop, *c.* 1930.

Standing outside Patterson's butcher shop in 1978 are, left to right: Fred Patterson, Tommy Neadle, Anthony Bowles.

In this Cardiff docklands establishment in the 1920s one could have had a bowl of soup, roll and butter and a cup of coffee for just threepence.

At the junction of Bute Street and Custom House Street were, left to right: Globe Boot Stores, A. Thomas (tobacconist), A. Kastenberg (jeweller), S. Fishman (tobacconist), Burts Leatherware, *c.* 1920.

This view is looking north along Bute Street. The building on the left of picture is the Chinese Seamen's Home, *c.* 1903.

Reese & Gwillim's grocery stores, James Street, *c.* 1914.

Pictured third from the left is shipowner Mr Ralph Elliot Morel. He was a keen sportsman and his racing colours, of red, white and black hoops, were taken from the funnel of the family shipping line. Second left is Tom Morel, chairman of the company, *c.* 1928.

A popular figure in Cardiff's dockland for more than forty years was Tommy Letton who later had a road named after him, *c.* 1950.

Tommy Letton sorting out the fish at Snowdens in Dumballs Road, *c.* 1950.

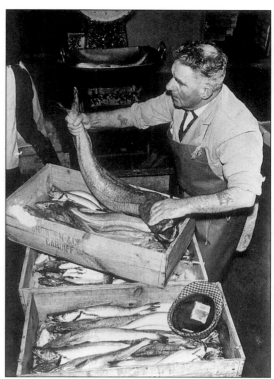

This was one fish that did not end up on Tommy's wheelbarrow, *c.* 1950.

A multitude of traders operated in Bute Street when this picture was taken around 1910.

Unemployed seamen hang around Corys Buildings in the hope of finding work, c. 1950. This corner was nicknamed Penniless Point.

Businessmen meet to discuss the day's dealings outside the Coal and Shipping Exchange in Mount Stuart Square in 1891.

More atmospheric scenes around the steps of the Coal and Shipping Exchange in 1891. The Exchange was built in 1886 at a cost of £40, 000.

Three
Streets and Buildings

A view of Butetown, looking north. The City Hall clock tower can be seen in the centre background, *c.* 1964.

The Pilotage Building in Stuart Street is to the left of this picture, *c.* 1898.

The Windsor Arms, on South William Street, is on the right of this picture and to the right of the lamp-post is the Museum Vaults, *c.* 1898.

These children play with their skipping ropes in Bute Esplanade. Numbers 8 to 12 were demolished when the Mount Stuart Dry Dock was extended.

Loudoun Square, *c.* 1957.

The building to the right of this picture of James Street is Merthyr House, c. 1920.

Looking south from Mount Stuart Square, c. 1930.

Bute Street looking towards the north, *c.* 1949.

The poster in the window of No. 7 Bute Terrace reads 'Vote Labour', *c.* 1945.

St Mary's church, Loudoun Square, is to the left of the picture, *c.* 1930.

Loudoun Square, *c.* 1950.

A view of Bute Street; note the overhead trolleybus cables, *c.* 1950. Owing to the height of the railway bridge at the north end of Bute Street, only single deck vehicles could be used.

The Salvation Army men's hostel on the corner of North Church Street and Bute Street, *c.* 1950.

Stuart Street looking east from Dudley Street, *c.* 1970.

Houses being demolished in Loudoun Square, *c.* 1957. In this year a five-year programme to clear 460 houses in Butetown was approved by Cardiff City Council.

A little boy posing for a picture in Loudoun Square in the late 1950s. An unlucky three-year-old child drowned in the fountain here in 1890.

A lithograph of the West Dock and site of Dock Chambers, c. 1890.

A detail from one of the walls on the Pier Head Building. The carved motto reads, 'Wrth Ddwr a Than' (By Water and Fire) proclaiming the triumph of steam power.

The Pier Head building, on the right of this picture, opened as the headquarters of the Cardiff Railway Company in 1897.

Powell Duffryn House, formerly the Merchants Exchange, was demolished after a fire in 1892.

The Customs and Excise House, Cardiff Docks, *c.* 1960.

The Royal Hamadryad Hospital in Ferry Road was opened in 1905.

The 7th Defence Force was billeted in the old barracks building in Burt Street during the First World War. A residential home now occupies the site.

The Sailors' Home in Stuart Street was financed by the Marquess of Bute. The drawing above shows the home, probably soon after it opened in 1856 and the photograph below shows it again in the early years of this century.

The John Cory Sailors and Soldiers Rest, at No. 179–80 Bute Street. It was built in 1902.

The John Cory Sailors and Soldiers Rest, c. 1903.

Patrons made use of the rest's facilities and took the opportunity to write home to loved ones, c. 1903.

A game of billiards is in progress here but most eyes are on the photographer, *c.* 1903.

The snooker room at the Seamen's Institute, *c.* 1903.

The Glamorgan Canal ran under James Street Bridge. Opened in 1794 as a means of transporting iron from Merthyr, it is hard to believe now that the canal was once a picturesque feature of old Cardiff. The last barge passed down the canal in 1942.

Clarence Road Bridge was opened by the Duke of Clarence in 1890. Note the 'Welcome' banner.

Eleanor Place, with Bertha Hughes' corner shop, *c.* 1973.

Eleanor Street, *c.* 1973.

Stuart Street in about 1973. A coal lorry can be seen outside the Windsor Arms.

The east side of Louisa Street, *c.* 1973.

A view of the east side of Adelaide Street taken from Stuart Street. The French Fried Fish shop is to the right of the picture, *c*. 1973.

The east side of Adelaide Street from James Street, *c*. 1973.

The west side of South William Street from James Street, *c.* 1973.

The west side of South William Street from Stuart Street, *c.* 1973.

Dudley Place was in a run down condition by the time this picture was taken around 1973.

Whatever became of these two little girls seen playing in Dudley Street in 1973?

The west side of Louisa Street from James Street, c. 1973.

The north side of Margaret Street from the western end, c. 1973.

The west side of George Street from Stuart Street, *c.* 1973.

Bute Street from the end of Stuart Street, *c.* 1973.

Four
Public Houses

The gentlemen in the centre of the middle row is Bob Downey who was the landlord of the Bute Castle Hotel which stood on the corner of Nelson Street and Angelina Street, *c.* 1925.

The Old Sea Lock Hotel was situated at the Glamorgan Canal Basin, *c*. 1891.

The New Sea Lock Hotel, Harrowby Street, *c*. 1950.

The Albion Hotel in Bute Street had a licence back in 1847. Landlady Nellie Collins served her last pint there in 1906, when these pictures were taken. The following year the premises became a boarding house.

The earliest record found that mentions the North & South Wales Hotel in Louisa Street dates from 1892.

The White Swan Inn, Bute Street, was closed in 1909.

The Windsor Hotel in Stuart Street, *c.* 1960. This was a well-known hotel and had many famous visitors including: Noel Coward, Katharine Hepburn, Henry Williamson, Daniel Farson, Kenneth Moore, Hugh Griffiths and Gwyn Thomas.

Once a coach house with stabling for two horses, The Ship & Pilot in James Street had a licence as early as 1861. It was refurbished in 1964, around the time this picture was taken.

Cardiff Castle Hotel, George Street, *c.* 1950.

Ye Olde Pilot Inn dated back to 1855 but had closed down by the time this picture was taken.

Another pub which dated back to 1855 was The White Hart Hotel, James Street. This view was taken around 1958.

The Packet Hotel, Bute Street, c. 1957.

A view of The Mount Stuart which was just outside the dock gates in Bute Crescent, *c.* 1970. The Mount Stuart was the first port of call for seamen and dockers. This coach house, in 1889, had fourteen bedrooms and stabling for nine horses.

The West Bute Dock Hotel in West Bute Street is now known as The Jug & Platter and is seen here around 1980.

The Pembroke Castle in Louisa Street was established in 1881. There was also a Pembroke Castle in Frederick Street at around the same time.

In the 1960s, people would visit the Quebec in Crichton Street to be entertained by Vic Parker the well-known guitarist.

The Custom House in Bute Street was situated, at one time, just ten yards away from another public house called The German Harp.

Five
Religion

James Walsh, headteacher of St Cuthbert's school, received the papal medal from the Archbishop of Cardiff, John Murphy, on the occasion of his retirement in 1975.

The Mission to the seaman's church, Bute West Dock, *c.* 1930.

The nave of this large church.

The opening of Peel Street mosque in 1947.

Peel Street mosque members posed outside the City Hall for this picture after the opening.

Peel Street mosque, *c.* 1950.

Molly Power, of St Cuthbert's school, is seen here in her confirmation dress. Now known as Molly Maher, she is the Butetown History and Arts Centre's archivist.

On 14 November 1920 a memorial plaque was unveiled at St Mary's church, Butetown, which was dedicated to those members of the parish who fell in the First World War.

The high altar in St Mary's church, c. 1930.

Members of the Greek Orthodox church in Butetown posed for this picture in the 1920s.

Muslims celebrated a holy day with a procession through the streets of Butetown in the 1950s.

80

St Paul's Methodist church, Loudoun
Square, *c.* 1930.

St Stephen's church, Mount Stuart
Square, *c.* 1960. The last service
was held there in 1975.

Norwegian seamen carried Cardiff's coal all over the world. The Norwegian Seaman's Mission stood on the eastern side of the West Bute Dock from 1866 to 1959. The present day replica (seen here) of the church shows it as it was from 1889.

Six
Schooldays

Eleanor Street school was built in 1878 and demolished in 1973. It was the first council school to be built in Cardiff.

Among the Eleanor Street school pupils in this picture are Leonard Day, Bobby Taylor and Billy Lewis, c. 1955.

Eleanor Street school soccer team, 1955.

Eleanor Street school pupils on a trip to London, *c.* 1955.

Eleanor Street school soccer players in the 1955/56 season. On the left is Raymond Ellard and on the right is John Perks. But who is the young man holding the ball?

Here are some pupils from Clarence Road school, c. 1932. Dot Dare, Jim Cowley, Ivor Amery and Bobby Mount are among these pupils.

Clarence Road school infants class, *c.* 1924.

Class 1 infants from Clarence Road school are seen here with teacher Miss Matthews (left) and headmistress Mrs Newton (right), *c.* 1916.

Somewhere in this picture of St Cuthbert's school, around 1931, are Wilf Glover, Arthur Jones, Joan Brett and Charlie Davey.

St Cuthbert's schoolteacher, Miss O' Reilly, is standing at the back on the extreme right in this photograph from around 1932.

Giving a helping hand at St Cuthbert's school fête are, left to right: Shirley Woodgate, Eileen Vaughn and Gwen Power, *c.* 1972.

The stall organizer for St Cuthbert's school fête, Peter Maher, is seen standing to the right at the back of this picture.

The combined soccer team of St Cuthbert's and St Paul's is seen here. Coach Charlie Cammelleri is on the back row, left, and teacher Mrs Jones is standing to the right of him. The goalkeeper is Richard Maher and the team was captained by Peter Bowden, c. 1981.

Richard Maher, Michelle Ugarte and Glyn Owen were among the St Cuthbert's school pupils in this group photograph taken around 1980.

South Church Street school broadcast party, c. 1938.

A group picture of South Church Street school. The boy extreme left is Alf Ashton, c. 1932.

South Church Street school, *c.* 1930. Joan Mazo, Nora Glasgow, Maime Freeman and George Phillips are among the pupils in the picture.

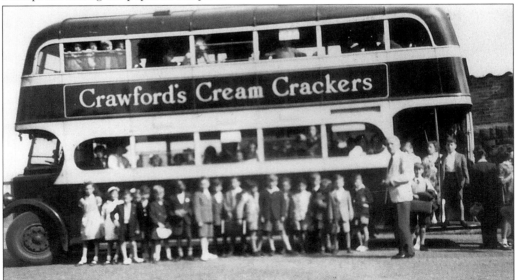

An Eleanor Street school outing, *c.* 1955.

South Church Street school rugby team, 1948/9 season.

St Mary the Virgin primary school nursery class, 1983.

Butetown children enjoy a kick around in front of the new tower blocks of flats, *c*. 1970.

Docklands children at play, *c*. 1955.

St Cuthbert's children line up for the Corpus Christi procession, *c.* 1970. The lady on the left is the teacher Kathy O'Reilly. Also in the picture are headteacher James Walsh (wearing spectacles), and on the extreme right is Tony Lloyd.

These Butetown children may be in their pyjamas, but they don't look a bit sleepy!

A rich mix of cultures is evident in this group of children celebrating the end of the Second World War in Loudoun Square. Among them are Maureen Jemmet, Iris and Clara Graham, Hamid and Derhim Radman, Pamela Acti, Ali Dobela, Billy Purvo, Mike Miller, Ahmed Omar.

The same celebrations and the girls in the bathing costumes are Pearl McLlquam (left) and Iris Williams (right).

Seven

Special Occasions

The coronation visit of King George V and Queen Mary on 25 June 1912. George V had been crowned the previous year.

The use of imported labour resulted in the National Sailors and Firemen's Union calling a strike in 1911. These cigar girls, who worked at Freemans, risked their jobs by coming out in sympathy.

The laying of the last stone of Roath Dock in 1887.

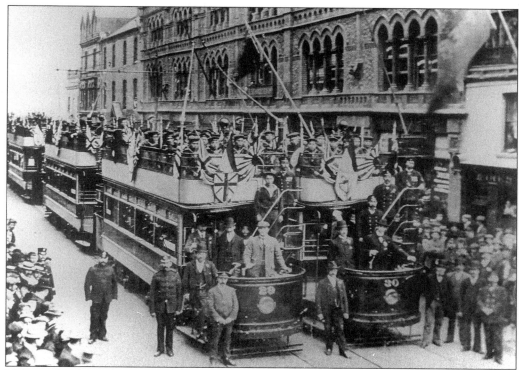

Thousands of people flocked to the docks to see the ships *Takasago* and *Asama* come into Cardiff in 1902, with nine hundred Japanese soldiers aboard.

A tram operating on the No. 6 route from Cathedral Road to Clarence Road can be seen here crossing Clarence Bridge. Opened by the Duke of Clarence in 1890, it was replaced in 1976.

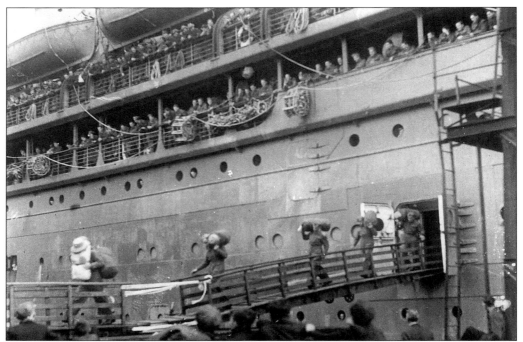

Troops disembarking from the SS *Rangitiki* at Cardiff Docks in November 1942.

The Home Guard and Civil Defence were inspected at Cardiff Docks in September 1943.

Coach outings were popular with the Butetown folk in the 1920s and '30s.

A Butetown coach outing, *c.* 1930.

Butetown Carnival, *c.* 1988.

The Adamant Jazz Band, with their major-domo Peter Phillips, often play at Butetown funerals.

The Mardi Gras Marching Band, *c.* 1968.

The Butetown Carnival celebrations, seen here in 1988, continue to attract thousands of people each year.

The inhabitants of Louisa Street held a party to celebrate George V's Silver Jubilee in 1935.

The 1959 thriller, *Tiger Bay*, starring John Mills, his daughter Hayley and Horst Buchholtz was made in the Cardiff Docks area. This critically acclaimed film was directed by J. Lee Thompson.

Harry Cooke, docklands poet, writer and old seadog, is seen here sitting in front of the ancient tree he saved from destruction by running in front of the bulldozers in 1993.

In the 1960s, television personality Bruce Forsyth (third left) visited the Rainbow Club in Butetown.

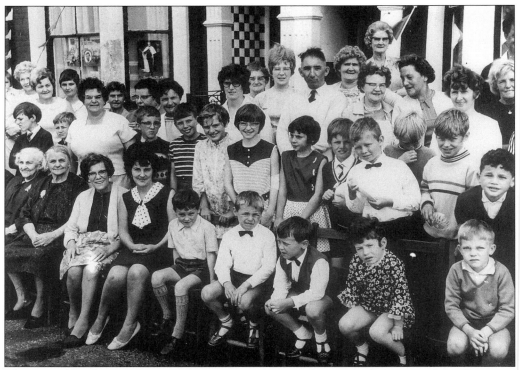

These Docklands neighbours pose for street photographs on the occasion of the Prince of Wales' investiture in 1969.

Another picture of people celebrating the Prince of Wales' investiture.

The Christmas dinner party was held at St Stephen's church hall in the 1950s. Tommy Letton's wife, Olive, used to organize trips and parties for local people, collecting weekly contributions of 1/6d for adults and 9d for children.

Father Christmas (Tommy Letton) arrives at St Stephen's church hall with presents for all the children, *c.* 1950.

Butetown residents pose for a picture in St Stephen's church hall before tucking in to their Christmas dinner, *c.* 1950.

In the 1960s members of the Butetown Youth Centre entertained the local community. Patty Boston, Eleanor Boston, Arthur Hedges and Elaine Campbell are somewhere in the picture.

A Welcome Mission outing, *c.* 1950.

Cardiff's Shirley Bassey was presented with a bouquet by members of the Rainbow Club in 1957. 'Shirley's surprise at her reception was so great the she began to cry. She was still weeping when a little dark girl, her hair arranged in plaits on top of her head, handed her a huge bouquet of lilies and roses.' (*Shirley: An Appreciation of the Life of Shirley Bassey* by Muriel Burgess.)

Shirley Bassey on another visit to the Rainbow Club in the early 1960s.

Eight
Sport

Cardiff International Athletic Club was unbeaten during the 1951/2 season. Left to right, standing: Johnny Martin, Len Fox, Wilf Rogers, John Actie, Arthur Holley, Windsor George (referee). Seated: Alec Neil, Frank Hooley, 'Bazza' Murphy, Harry Ernest, Sammy John. Front row: Johnny Thomas, Billy Boston, George Percy (capt), Basil Roderick, Danny James. Johnny Martin emigrated to Canada and became mayor of his new town.

Billy Boston, the boy from Tiger Bay, was destined to become someone special in the world of rugby. This was obvious from his early years, but it was not in his homeland that he found real fame. Billy B was snapped up by Wigan for £3,000, in 1953, to launch a dazzling Rugby League career that spanned seventeen years and saw him score 571 tries – more than any other British player. He was a star of the Welsh Boys' Clubs XV, as a full back against England, and won his expected Welsh Youth Cap. Billy, at eighteen years old, became the youngest captain to lead Cardiff and District RU XV in the traditional opening match against Cardiff at the Arms Park. He thundered over for 126 tries in 30 games in one season for the Royal Signals and piled up 37 points in his first match for them. Aged nineteen, he was in the Great Britain team which toured 'Down Under'. He weighed 12st 8lb. A master of swerve and the hammer-blow hand-off, he was capable of impressive speed and he soon became recognized as one of the greatest Rugby League entertainers of all time.

I was the first to write about Billy when he played for Cardiff International Athletic Club, the famous CIACs, and he featured prominently in the rugby columns of the *Cardiff Times*. Billy B appeared a few times for Neath before the Rugby League scouts swooped and Wigan won the race for his signature. Boston was the son of a West Indian father and Irish mother, born in Butetown, and was one of seven children. He attended South Church Street school, Tiger Bay, where Gus Risman, Johnny Freeman and Colin Dixon received their early education before 'matriculating' to the hall of Rugby League fame. The CIACs, a Cardiff and District Rugby Union club, were proud of their reputation of being open to all colours and creeds and enjoyed an unbeaten record in 1951/2 with Boston a key performer.

John Billot
Former Sports Editor of *The Western Mail*

Gus Risman attended South Church Street school. Augustus John Risman joined Salford RL Club in 1929 for £152, payable over the year. A supreme tactician with the uncanny vision to create tries from his favourite full back position, he scored more than 3,000 points for Salford as one of the game's greatest goal kickers. He played for Great Britain against Australia aged thirty-five and was forty-one years old when he figured in the Workington Town team in the RL Challenge Cup final at Wembley.

Cardiff Loudouns Rugby Club in the 1920/1 season.

The Coloured International Cricket Club, 1923.

Butetown cricket team, c. 1950.

Docks United AFC were League Champions and Lennard Cup winners in 1947/8. Left to right, back row: E. Emery, H. Perks, F. Johnson. T. Mansbridge, E, Mansbridge, W. Dite, T. Letton. Middle row: B. Rudd, T. Carey, A. Stephenson, L. Ford, J. Ugarte (capt.), W. East, E. Johnson, E. Taylor. Front row: G. Carey, D. Mackie, R. Griffiths, C. Skuse.

Docks United Juniors, 1947/8. Left to right, back row: P. Mansbridge (trainer), K. Jeffries, D. Hughes, C. Lewis, R. Taylor, V. Pearson, W. Taylor, T. Letton (treasurer). Front row: B. Clifton, O. Brahm, S. Cleary, L. Reece, R. Laverick.

Among the members of St Cuthbert's school baseball team are: John Fletcher, John Guilford, Eddie Barry, Laurie Brahim, *c.* 1950.

Eleanor Street soccer team in the 1953/4 season.

South Wales Echo boxing correspondent David Phillips (left) shares a joke with local boxers Joe Eskine and Phil Edwards.

Cardiff City's Phil Dwyer is seen here with St Cuthbert's winning baseball team which included Andrew Lucas, Richard Maher and Glyn Owen, *c.* 1981.

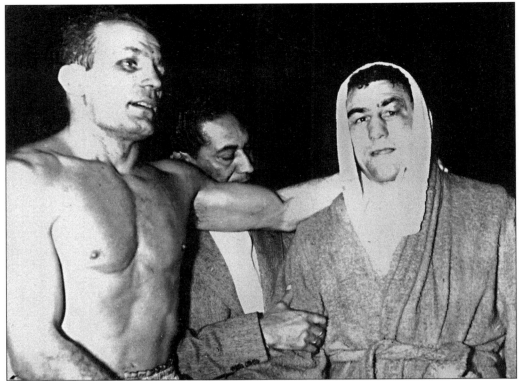

Henry Cooper (left) and Joe Erskine (right) fought each other on a number of occasions and still remained the best of pals.

Mount Stuart Dry Dock rugby team, c. 1958. Three of the players were Neil O' Halleran, Roger Pleece and Alan Hawkey.

Members of Butetown Youth Club show off their trophies. Among them are Brian Mohamed, Darren Acti, Russell Thompson and Calvin Chew, *c.* 1983.

Cardiff International Athletic Club was unbeaten during the 1951/2 season. To the left of the Lord Mayor of Cardiff, Sir James Collins (centre), is Welsh rugby international Bleddyn Williams, wearing a striped tie and blazer.

The Welsh Sports Hall of Fame at the South Glamorgan County Council building at Cardiff Bay was opened by former Wigan and Great Britain Rugby League player Billy Boston on 3 February 1989. Also in the picture is Councillor W.P. 'Paddy' Kitson. There are a number of rugby players on the Welsh Sports Hall of Fame's roll of honour list and these include: Billy Boston, Gerald Davies, Cliff Jones, Ken Jones, Cliff Morgan, Jim Sullivan, J.P.R. Williams. These days the Welsh Sports Hall of Fame is situated at the Welsh Folk Museum, St Fagan's, Cardiff.

Nine
The Rainbow Club

The Rainbow Club's 'Save The Children' display.

Rainbow Club children gather at the Cardiff Central railway station to welcome international singing star Shirley Bassey in 1957.

Putting the finishing touches to the cake baked for Shirley Bassey's visit to the Rainbow Club, in 1957.

Rainbow Club children in Welsh national costume, 1957.

International cabaret singer Patti Flynn from Butetown is seen here modelling one of Shirley Bassey's many dresses, c. 1960.

The
RAINBOW CLUB
A Photographic Exhibition of Bay Heritage

Over 20 years
of Childrens' Fun

15th June - July
1997

Butetown History & Arts Centre

Pages reproduced from a Butetown History and Arts Centre leaflet.

Butetown History & Arts Centre

Opening Hours:
Thurs, Fri, Sat & Sun. 11.30am - 4.30pm
Free Admission

5 Dock Chambers,
Bute Street, Cardiff. CF1 6AG
Tel: 01222 494757 Fax: 01222 255887

Registered in Wales. Company No. 3306029. Registered Charity No. 1060986

CARDIFF BAY

Front Cover Picture : courtesy of the South Wales Echo

Fifty years ago a childrens' club was started in a disused shop in Bute Street. It was situated near the Cairo Cafe owned by Mr and Mrs Salaman. Originally named the Play Centre, the club was started by Mr John, a member of the Society of Friends and a teacher at Cardiff High School. The Save the Children Fund accepted responsibility for the club in 1947.

During the 1950s and 1960s the club was run by Mr and Mrs Capener. Mr Capener, who owned and ran a travel bureau in Queen Street, was the County Youth Organiser. Mrs Capener, born in Merthyr, was an active youth worker. She was also a former Cambridge scholar and schoolteacher. Both the Capeners were well known and well respected within the community. Mrs Salaman remembers Mr Capener as being a very quiet reserved man,

whereas Mrs Capener was a very outg forthright and determined lady.

The club was named the Rainbow Club bec children of 25 different nationalities atter forming a 'multitude of nations'. From Mc to Friday it provided a nightly meeting for children from 8 years upwards. Mr G Ernest remembers going to the club two r each week to teach boxing and also super the children in different classes. There v carpentry shop for the boys and coo classes for the girls. The children also p table tennis, billiards and draughts. Sp outings were arranged, including trips tc seaside.

Arguably the most famous member of the was Shirley Bassey dubbed the 'Tigress the Bay' by the press. Gerald Ernest remem

club

Theme:
'Multitude of Nations' children of 25 different
nationalities attended the Rainbow Club.

Mr. & Mrs. Capener
who organised the activities in the club

norous evening dress donated to the club
irley Bassey, hanging in the hall. Some of
irls used to try it on, but found it too heavy
ear.

embership of the Rainbow Club grew new
ises were needed and in 1956 the former
iff Soldiers and Sailors Rest at 246 Bute
t was taken over. The club became firmly
lished in Butetown and was well
orted by parents.

Salaman remembers how much the
en loved it and looked forward to going.
lso recalls the strong sense of community
the area at that time.

lived in Bute Street, supposedly one of the
ost notorious areas in Cardiff but I never
w anything bad. You were not classed as

an 'ethnic group' in those days, just part of
one's community regardless of religion, race
or colour, just one big family. I never wanted
to leave".

In 1968 the club was still in existence, and the
premises were refurbished to celebrate the
Save the Children Fund's 21st anniversary of
its work at the Rainbow Club.

The photographs on display at the Butetown
History & Art Centre in Bute Street form part
of a collection mainly taken by Mr Malcolm
Capener and donated to BHAC by his friend
Mr Grey when Mr Capener died. They form
part of a large collection of archival material
which documents the rich and unique history
of Britains most famous multi-cultural
community of 'Tiger Bay and the Docks'.

127

Members of the Rainbow Club aboard the HMS *Tiger*, October 1966.

Acknowledgements

First of all we would like to thank the Rt Hon. Alun Michael JP, MP, Secretary of State for Wales and Honorary President of Butetown History and Arts Centre, for writing the foreword. Special thanks to the editors of the *South Wales Echo*, *Western Mail* and *Cardiff Post* for publishing requests to readers for photographs and for giving permission to use several items from their own picture library.

For the loan of photographs, and permission to use them, we are greatly indebted to the following people: John Billot (former sports editor of *Western Mail*, who also wrote the piece on Billy Boston), BHAC Archive, *Western Mail & Echo*, Mrs Rene Ussell, Mrs Sheila Thomas, Mrs Jackson, Mr Chelmis, Mrs Carpenter, Mrs Gardener, Allen Hambly, Phil Street, Philip Hall, Dave of Salisbury Antiques and Mr Bob Evans. Also Paul Dunleavy, Idris Bowen, Jim Cowley, Mr Griffiths, Reg Crabtree, Alan Hawkley and the late Malcolm Capener.

Others we need to thank are the staff of the Cardiff Central Library Local History Department for their help, and especially James Lee Harvey for typing the text and captions.

We would also like to thank those people who offered photographs, poems, reminiscences, etc., which, for lack off space, were not used. Finally we ask forgiveness of any contributors who may have been omitted from these acknowledgements.